DIDO & ÆNEAS

HENRY PURCELL

Libretto by/*Libretto von*
Nahum Tate

Edited by/*Herausgegeben von*
Edward J. Dent

Revised Edition by/*Revidierte Ausgabe von*
Ellen T. Harris

German translation by/*Deutsche Übersetzung von*
A. Meyer

CHORUS SCORE / *CHORPARTITUR*

The complete vocal score and the full score are also on sale
Die Partitur und vollständige Klavierpartitur sind ebenfalls käuflich erhältlich

DIDO AND AENEAS

Nahum Tate
(1652–1712)

edited by Edward J. Dent and Ellen T. Harris

Henry Purcell
(1659–1695)

Chorus Score

3

BELINDA

bless-ing___Fate can give, Our Car-thage to se-cure, and Troy___re-vive. When
Glück Ge-schick uns lenkt, Kartha-go gleich wie___Tro-ja neu___ge-schenkt. Wenn

[♩.=♩]

mon-archs u-nite, how hap-py their state, They tri-umph at once o'er their
Herr-scher ver-eint, wie gross ist ihr Glück, Sie la-chen zu-gleich ü-ber

foes and their fate, they triumph, they tri-umph at once o'er their foes and their fate.
Feind und Ge-schick, sie la-chen, sie la-chen zu-gleich ü-ber Feind und Ge-schick.

BELINDA & SECOND WOMAN

Fear no dan - ger__ to en - sue, The he - ro loves as well as you.
Fürcht' nicht, dass Ge - fahr er - schien, Dein Held liebt Dich so wie Du ihn.

CHORUS

[f-p]

Fear no dan - ger__ to en - sue, The he - ro loves as well as you.
Fürcht' nicht, dass Ge - fahr er - schien, Dein Held liebt Dich so wie Du ihn.

[f-p]

[1st time for.]
2nd time pia.

[f-p]

[p]

S. 1.
2.

Ev - er gen - tle, ev - er smil - ing, And the cares of life be - guil - ing,
Vol - ler Froh - sinn, im - mer hei - ter, Kümmern Sor - gen ihn nicht wei - ter,

A.

[p]
pia.

6

Fear no dan-ger___ to en-sue, The he-ro loves as well as you.
Fürcht' nicht, dass Ge-fahr er-schien, Dein Held liebt Dich so wie Du ihn

for.

Cu-pid strew your path with flowers, Ga-ther'd from E-ly-sian bowers.
A-mor streut den Pfad mit Blü-ten, Die sie im E-ly-sium hü-ten

Fear no dan-ger___ to en-sue, The he-ro loves as well as you.
Fürcht' nicht, dass Ge-fahr er-schien, Dein Held liebt Dich so wie Du ihn

Dance this Cho[rus]. The Baske.
Tanzen während des Gesangs. Baskische Tanz.

8

40

46

14

mis - chief all our skill, _____ and mis - chief, mis - chief all our skill.
Un - heil lässt uns ruhn, _____ kein Un - heil, Un - heil lässt uns ruhn

_____ and mis - chief all our skill, and mis - chief, mis - chief all our skill.
_____ kein Un - heil lässt uns ruhn, kein Un - heil, Un - heil lässt uns ruhn

mis - chief all our skill, and _____ mis - chief, mis - chief, mis - chief all our skill.
Un - heil lässt uns ruhn, kein _____ Un - heil, Un - heil, Un - heil lässt uns ruhn

_____ and mis - chief all _____ our skill, and mis - chief all our skill.
_____ kein Un - heil lässt _____ uns ruhn, kein Un - heil lässt uns ruhn

SORCERESS

The Queen of Car - thage, whom we hate, As we do
Kar - tha - gos Her - rin, sehr ver - hasst, Wie al - le

(V.S.)

all in _____ pros - p'rous state, Ere sun - set shall most
Fro - hen _____ uns zur Last, Vor A - bend nichts ihr

ho ho ho ho ho ho ho ho ho ho ho ho ho!

FIRST WITCH

SECOND WITCH

Ru - in'd ere the set of sun? Tell us, tell us, tell us,
Heut' schon, eh' die Son - ne sinkt? Sag uns, sag uns, sag uns,

ho ho ho ho ho ho ho ho ho ho ho ho ho ho ho

SECOND WITCH

ho ho ho ho ho ho ho ho ho ho ho ho ho ho ho ho!

But
Doch

Soft

prac - tice, for___ this o - pen___ air, for___ this___ o - pen___ air.
-len - den, für___ son - ni - ge___ Luft, für___ son - ni - ge___ Luft.

Eccho Dance. Inchantresses and Fairies
Echotanz. Hexen und Feen

(Echo Dance of Furies)
(Echotanz der Furien)

24

28 Gitter ground a Dance

Gitarrentanz. (Chaconne).

21

haste, haste, haste, haste _____ to _____ town.
schnell, schnell, schnell, schnell _____ zur _____ Stadt.

haste, haste, haste, haste, haste _____ to town.
schnell, schnell, schnell, schnell _____ zur Stadt.

haste, haste, haste, haste, haste, haste to town.
schnell, schnell, schnell, schnell, schnell, schnell zur Stadt.

haste, haste, haste, haste, haste, haste, haste to town.
schnell, schnell, schnell, schnell, schnell, schnell, schnell zur Stadt.

The Spirit of the Sorceress descends to Aeneas in likeness of Mercury.
Das Gespenst der Zauberinnen herabsteigt vor Aeneas in der Gestalt des Merkurys.

32

SPIRIT

Stay, Prince, and hear great Jove's _____ com - mand. He summons thee this night a -
Halt Fürst! und hör Zeus' Wort _____ zu Dir. Heut' Nacht noch musst Du fort von

more, no, nev-er, no, nev-er in-tend-ing to____ vis - it them more.
Strand, auch wenn ihr nie wie-der-seht, wie-der-seht____ hier____ die-sen Strand.

The Sailors Dance
Matrosentanz

Jack of the Lanthorn leads the Spaniards out of their way among the Inchantresses. A Dance.
Jack von Lanthorn (ein Nachtwächter) führt die Spanier zwischen die Hexen. Ein Tanz.

(The Witches Dance)
(Hexentanz)

Cupids appear in the Clouds o'er her Tomb
Nymphen erscheinen in den Wolken über ihrem Grab

With droop - ing wings ye Cu - pids come, with droop - - - ing wings, with
In sanft - em Flug, oh kommt her-ab, in sanft - - - em Flug, in

With droop - ing wings ye
In sanft - em Flug, oh

With droop - ing wings ye Cu - pids come, with droop - ing,
In sanft - em Flug, oh kommt her - ab, in sanft - em,

With droop - ing wings ye Cu - pids come,
In sanft - em Flug, oh kommt her - ab,

38

Cupids' Dance
Amorettentanz
[2nd time instruments only]

FINIS